JACK KEROUAC

Scattered Poems

POCKET POET SERIES #28

City Lights Books
San Francisco

Some of these poems have appeared 1945-1970 in *Ark*, *Beetitood*,
Berkeley Bussei, *Chicago Review*, *Combustion*, *The Floating Bear*,
Jester of Columbia, *Kriya Press Broadsides*, *The Lowell House Printers
Broadsides*, *Metronome*, *Neurotica*, *New Departures*, *New Directions*,
The Outsider, *Pax Broadsides*, *Playboy*, *Portents*, *Red Clay Reader*,
TriQuarterly, *Variegation*, *White Dove Review*, and *Yugen*. The poems
were selected from these sources and unpublished mss. by
Ann Charters.

Cover photo of Jack Kerouac by William S. Burroughs
(Tangier, 1957)

City Lights Books are available to bookstores through our
primary distributor: Subterranean Company, Box 168,
265 S. 5th Street, Monroe, Oregon 97456. 1-503-847-5274.
Toll-free orders 1-800-274-7826. FAX 503-847-6018. Our
books are also available through library jobbers and regional
distributors. For personal orders and catalogs, please write to
City Lights Books, 261 Columbus Avenue, San Francisco,
CA 94133.

CITY LIGHTS BOOKS are edited by Lawrence Ferlinghetti
and Nancy J. Peters and published at the City Lights Bookstore,
261 Columbus Avenue, San Francisco, CA 94133.

CONTENTS

CONTENTS (Continued)

The new American poetry as typified by the SF Renaissance (which means Ginsberg, me, Rexroth, Ferlinghetti, McClure, Corso, Gary Snyder, Philip Lamantia, Philip Whalen, I guess) is a kind of new-old Zen Lunacy poetry, writing whatever comes into your head as it comes, poetry returned to its origin, in the bardic child, truly ORAL as Ferling said, instead of gray faced Academic quibbling. Poetry & prose had for long time fallen into the false hands of the false. These new pure poets confess forth for the sheer joy of confession. They are CHILDREN. They are also childlike graybeard Homers singing in the street. They SING, they SWING. It is diametrically opposed to the Eliot shot, who so dismally advises his dreary negative rules like the objective correlative, etc. which is just a lot of constipation and ultimately emasculation of the pure masculine urge to freely sing. In spite of the dry rules he set down his poetry is itself sublime. I could say lots more but aint got time or sense. But SF is the poetry of a new Holy Lunacy like that of ancient times (Li Po, Hanshan, Tom O Bedlam, Kit Smart, Blake) yet it also has that mental discipline typified by the haiku (Basho, Buson), that is, the discipline of pointing out things directly, purely, concretely, no abstractions or explanations, wham wham the true blue song of man.

Jack Kerouac — THE ORIGINS OF JOY IN POETRY

A TRANSLATION FROM THE FRENCH OF JEAN-LOUIS INCOGNITEAU*

My beloved who wills not to love me:
My life which cannot love me:
I seduce both.

She with my round kisses . . .
(In the smile of my beloved the approbation of the cosmos)
Life is my art . . .
(Shield before death)
Thus without sanction I live.
(What unhappy theodicy!)

One knows not—
One desires—
      Which is the sum.

Allen Ginsberg
*(Kerouac translated by Ginsberg)

1945

Song: FIE MY FUM

Pull my daisy,
Tip my cup,
Cut my thoughts
For coconuts,

Start my arden
Gate my shades,
Silk my garden
Rose my days,

Say my oops,
Ope my shell,
Roll my bones,
Ring my bell,

Pope my parts,
Pop my pot,
Poke my pap,
Pit my plum.

Allen Ginsberg & Jack Kerouac

1950

PULL MY DAISY

Pull my daisy
tip my cup
all my doors are open
Cut my thoughts
for coconuts
all my eggs are broken
Jack my Arden
gate my shades
woe my road is spoken
Silk my garden
rose my days
now my prayers awaken

Bone my shadow
dove my dream
start my halo bleeding
Milk my mind &
make me cream
drink me when you're ready
Hop my heart on
harp my height
seraphs hold me steady
Hip my angel
hype my light
lay it on the needy

Heal the raindrop
sow the eye
bust my dust again
Woe the worm
work the wise
dig my spade the same
Stop the hoax
what's the hex
where's the wake
how's the hicks
take my golden beam

Rob my locker
lick my rocks
leap my cock in school
Rack my lacks
lark my looks
jump right up my hole
Whore my door
beat my boor
eat my snake of fool
Craze my hair
bare my poor
asshole shorn of wool

say my oops
ope my shell

Bite my naked nut
Roll my bones
ring my bell
call my worm to sup
Pope my parts
pop my pot
raise my daisy up
Poke my pap
pit my plum
let my gap be shut

Allen Ginsberg, Jack Kerouac, Neal Cassady

1948-1950?
1961

PULL MY DAISY

Pull my daisy
Tip my cup
Cut my thoughts
for coconuts

Jack my Arden
Gate my shades
Silk my garden
Rose my days

Bone my shadow
Dove my dream
Milk my mind &
Make me cream

Hop my heart on
Harp my height
Hip my angel
Hype my light

Heal the raindrop
Sow the eye
Woe the worm
Work the wise

Stop the hoax
Where's the wake
What's the box
How's the Hicks

Rob my locker
Lick my rocks
Rack my lacks
Lark my looks

Whore my door
Beat my beer
Craze my hair
Bare my poor

Say my oops
Ope my shell
Roll my bones
Ring my bell

Pope my parts
Pop my pet
Poke my pap
Pit my plum

Allen Ginsberg, Jack Kerouac, Neal Cassady

1951, 1958?
1961

He is your friend, let him dream;
He's not your brother, he's not yr. father,
He's not St. Michael he's a guy.

He's married, he works, go on sleeping
On the other side of the world,
Go thinking in the Great European Night

I'm explaining him to you my way not yours,
Child, Dog, ——listen: go find your soul,
Go smell the wind, go far.

Life is a pity. Close the book, go on,
Write no more on the wall, on the moon,
At the Dog's, in the sea in the snowing bottom.

Go find God in the nights, the clouds too.
When can it stop this big circle at the skull
oh Neal; there are men, things outside to do.

Great huge tombs of Activity
in the desert of Africa of the heart,
The black angels, the women in bed

with their beautiful arms open for you
in their youth, some tenderness
Begging in the same shroud.

The big clouds of new continents,
O foot tired in climes so mysterious,
Don't go down the otherside for nothing.

1952?

Old buddy aint you gonna stay by me?
Didnt we say I'd die by a lonesome tree
And you come and dont cut me down
But I'm lying as I be
Under a deathsome tree
Under a headache cross
Under a powerful boss
Under a hoss
       (my kingdom for a hoss
         a hoss
      fork a hoss and head
      for ole Mexico)
Joe, aint you my buddy thee?
And stay by me, when I fall & die
In the apricot field
      And you, blue moon, what you doon
      Shining in the sky
      With a glass of port wine
      In your eye

——Ladies, let fall your drapes
and we'll have an evening
of interesting rapes
      inneresting rapes

1956?

DAYDREAMS FOR GINSBERG

I lie on my back at midnight
hearing the marvelous strange chime
of the clocks, and know it's mid-
night and in that instant the whole
world swims into sight for me
in the form of beautiful swarm-
ing m u t t a worlds——
everything is happening, shining
Buhudda-lands, bhuti
blazing in faith, I know I'm
forever right & all's I got to
do (as I hear the ordinary
extant voices of ladies talking
in some kitchen at midnight
oilcloth cups of cocoa
cardore to mump the
rinnegain in his
darlin drain——) i will write
it, all the talk of the world
everywhere in this morning, leav-
ing open parentheses sections
for my own accompanying inner
thoughts —— with roars of me
all brain—— all world
roaring——vibrating——I put
it down, swiftly, 1,000 words

(of pages) compressed into one second
of time —— I'll be long
robed & long gold haired in
the famous Greek afternoon
of some Greek City
Fame Immortal & they'll
have to find me where they find
the t h n u p f t of my
shroud bags flying
flag yagging Lucien
Midnight back in their
mouths —— Gore Vidal'll
be amazed, annoyed ——
   my words'll be writ in gold
& preserved in libraries like
Finnegans Wake & Visions of Neal

1955?

12

LUCIEN MIDNIGHT

Dying is ecstasy.
I'm not a teacher, not a
Sage, not a Roshi, not a
writer or master or even
a giggling dharma bum I'm
my mother's son & my mother
is the universe ――
   What is this universe
      but a lot of waves
   And a craving desire
      is a wave
   Belonging to a wave
      in a world of waves
   So why put any down,
      wave?
   Come on wave, WAVE!
   The heehaw's dobbin
      spring hoho
   Is a sad lonely yurk
      for your love
   Wave lover

And what is God?
The unspeakable, the untellable,
――

Rejoice in the Lamb, sang

Christopher Smart, who
drives me crazy, because
he's so smart, and I'm
so smart, and both of us
are crazy.

No, — what is God?
The impossible, the impeachable
Unimpeachable Prezi-dent
Of the Pepsodent Universe
But with no body & no brain
no business and no tie
no candle and no high
no wise and no smart guy
no nothing, no no-nothing,
no anything, no-word, yes-word,
  everything, anything, God,
  the guy that aint a guy,
  the thing that cant be
  and can
  and is
  and isnt

Kayo Mullins is always yelling
and stealing old men's shoes

Moon comes home drunk, kerplunk,
Somebody hit him with a pisspot

Major Hoople's always harrumfing
Egad kaff kaff all that
Showing little kids fly kites right
And breaking windows of fame

Blemish me Lil Abner is gone
His brother is okay, Daisy Mae
And the Wolf-Gal

    Ah who cares?
    Subjects make me sick
    all I want is C'est Foi
    Hope one time
    bullshit in the tree

I've had enough of follin me
And making silly imagery
    Harrumph me kaff
    I think I'll take off
    For Cat and fish

1957

1

Someday you'll be lying
there in a nice trance
and suddenly a hot
soapy brush will be
applied to your face
——it'll be unwelcome
——someday the
undertaker will shave you

2

Sweet monstranot love
By momma dears
Hey
Call God the Mother
To stop this fight

3

Me that repeated & petered
The meter & lost 2 cents

Me that was fined
To be hined
And refined
    Ay

Me that was
Whoo ee
The owl
On the fence

4

Old Navajoa shit dog, you,
your goodies are the goodiest
goodies I ever did see, how
dog you shore look mad
when yer bayin

Hoo Hound-dog!
    don't eat that dead rabbit
    in front of my face raw
    —— Cook it a lil bit

1953-4?
1968

I
  clearly
        saw
                the skeleton underneath
all
    this
        show
                of personality
what
        is
        left
                of a man and all his pride
but bones?
and all his lost snacks o' nights . . .
  and the bathtubs of liquor
    thru his gullet
                    . . . <u>bones</u> —— He mopes
                        in the grave,
                        facial features
                        changed by worms
                            *
                              *
                                *
                                  *
  from him
             is heard
                    no more

```
        *
      *
        *
          *
```

Life is sick
Dogs cough
Bees sail
Birds hack
Trees saw
Woods cry
Men die
Ticks try
Books lie
Ants fly
Goodbye

1960

HYMN

And when you showed me Brooklyn Bridge
  in the morning,
    Ah God,
And the people slipping on ice in the street,
twice,
        twice,
            two different people
            came over, goin to work,
            so earnest and tryful,
            clutching their pitiful
            morning Daily News
            slip on the ice & fall
            both inside 5 minutes
            and I cried I cried
That's when you taught me tears, Ah
  God in the morning,
    Ah Thee
And me leaning on the lamppost wiping
eyes,
      eyes,
            nobody's know I'd cried
            or woulda cared anyway
            but O I saw my father
            and my grandfather's mother
            and the long lines of chairs
            and tear-sitters and dead,

        Ah me, I knew God You
        had better plans than that
So whatever plan you have for me
Splitter of majesty
Make it short
  brief
Make it snappy
  bring me home to the Eternal Mother
  today
At your service anyway,
  (and until)

1959

POEM

I demand that the human race
ceases multiplying its kind
         and bow out
         I advise it

And as punishment & reward
for making this plea I know
         I'll be reborn
         the last human
Everybody else dead and I'm
an old woman roaming the earth
         groaning in caves
         sleeping on mats

And sometimes I'll cackle, sometimes
pray, sometimes cry, eat & cook
         at my little stove
         in the corner
"Always knew it anyway,"
         I'll say
And one morning won't get up from my mat

1962

THE THRASHING DOVES

In the back of the dark Chinese store
  in a wooden jailhouse bibbet box
  with dust of hay on the floor, rice
  where the rice bags are leaned,
  beyond the doomed peekokoos in the box
  cage

All the little doves'll die.
  As well as the Peekotoos——eels
  ——they'll bend chickens' necks back
  oer barrels and slice at Samsara
  the world of eternal suffering with silver
  blades as thin as the ice in Peking

As thick & penetrable as the Wall of China
  the rice darkness of that store, beans,
  tea, boxes of dried fish, doodlebones,
  pieces of sea-weed, dry, pieces of eight,
  all the balloon of the shroud on the floor

And the lights from little tinkly Washington St.
  Behung, dim, opium pipes and gong wars,
  Tong, the rice and the card game——and
  Tibbet de tibbet the tink tink tink
  them Chinese cooks do in the kitchen
  Jazz

The thrashing doves in the dark, white fear,
   my eyes reflect that liquidly
   and I no understand Buddha-fear?
   awakener's fear? So I give warnings
   'bout midnight round about midnight

And tell all the children the little otay
   story of magic, multiple madness, maya
   otay, magic trees-sitters and little girl
   bitters, and littlest lil brothers
   in crib made made of clay (blue in the moon).

For the doves.

1956?
1959

The Buddhist Saints are the incomparable saints
Wooing continue of lovemilk, mewling
And purling with lovely voices for love,
For perfect compassionate pity
Without making one false move
                    of action,

Perfectly accomodating commiserations
For all sentient belaboring things.
     Passive Sweetsaints
     Waiting for your Holyhood
     Hoping for your eventual join
     In their bright confraternity.

Perfect Divines. I can name some.
What's in a name. They were saints
Of the Religion of the Awakening
From the Dream of Existence
And Non-Existence.
                    They know that life and death
                    The knowing of life, muteness of death,
                    Are mutual dual twin opposites
                    Conceptioning on each side of the Truth
                    Which is the pivot in the Center
                    And which says: "Neither life
                    nor death — neither existence

nor non-existence — but the central
lapse and absence of them both."

1956?

HOW TO MEDITATE

                 ——lights out——
fall, hands a-clasped, into instantaneous
ecstasy like a shot of heroin or morphine,
the gland inside of my brain discharging
the good glad fluid (Holy Fluid) as
I hap-down and hold all my body parts
down to a deadstop trance — Healing
all my sicknesses — erasing all — not
even the shred of a "I-hope-you" or a
Loony Balloon left in it, but the mind
blank, serene, thoughtless. When a thought
comes a-springing from afar with its held-
forth figure of image, you spoof it out,
you spuff it off, you fake it, and
it fades, and thought never comes — and
with joy you realize for the first time
"Thinking's just like not thinking —
So I don't have to think
   any
   more"

1967

A PUN FOR AL GELPI

Jesus got mad one day
  at an apricot tree.
He said, "Peter, you
  of the Holy See,
Go see if the tree is ripe."
  "The tree is not yet ripe,"
  reported back Peter the Rock.
"Then let it wither!"
Jesus wanted an apricot.
In the morning, the tree
  had withered,
Like the ear in the agony
  of the garden,
Struck down by the sword.
  Unready.
  What means this parable?
Everybody
  better see.
You're really sipping
When your glass
  is always empty.

1966

SEPT. 16, 1961, POEM

How awfully sad I felt thinking of my sleeping mother in her
  bed
that she'll die someday
tho she herself says "death is nothing to worry about,
from this life we start to another"
How awfully sad I felt anyway ——
That have no wine to make me forget my rotting teeth is bad
  enough
but that my whole body is rotting and my mother's body is
  rotting
towards death, it's all so insanely sad.
I went outside in the pure dawn: but why should I be glad
  about
a dawn
that dawns on another rumor of war,
and why should I be sad: isnt the air at least pure and fresh?
I looked at the flowers on the bush: one of them had fallen:
another was just bloomed open: neither of them were sad or
  glad.
I suddenly realized all things just come and go
  including any feeling of sadness: that too will go:
  sad today glad tomorrow: somber today drunk tomorrow:
    why fret
    so much?
        Everybody in the world has flaws just like me.

Why should I put myself down? Which is a feeling just
coming to go.
Everything comes and goes. How good it is!
Evil wars wont stay forever!
Pleasant forms also go.
Since everything just comes and goes O why be
sad? or glad?
Sick today healthy tomorrow. But O I'm so
sad just the same!
Just coming and going all over the place,
the place itself coming and going.
We'll all end up in heaven anyway, together
in that golden eternal bliss I saw.
O how damned sad I cant write about it
well.
This is an attempt at the easy lightness
of Ciardian poetry.
I should really use my own way.
But that too will go, worries about
style. About sadness.
My little happy purring cat hates
doors!
And sometimes he's sad and silent,
hot nose, sighs,
and a little heartbroken mew.
There go the birds, flying west
a moment.

Who's going to ever know the
world before it goes?

1962

RIMBAUD

    Arthur!
      On t'appela pas Jean!
Born in 1854 cursing in Charle-
ville thus paving the way for
the abominable murderousnesses
of Ardennes —
No wonder your father left!
So you entered school at 8
— Proficient little Latinist you!
In October of 1869
Rimbaud is writing poetry
in Greek French —
Takes a runaway train

to Paris without a ticket,
the miraculous Mexican Brakeman
throws him off the fast
train, to Heaven, which
he no longer travels because
Heaven is everywhere —
Nevertheless the old fags
intervene —
Rimbaud nonplussed Rimbaud
trains in the green National
Guard, proud, marching
in the dust with his heroes —

hoping to be buggered,
dreaming of the ultimate Girl.
— Cities are bombarded as
he stares & stares & chews
his degenerate lip & stares
with gray eyes at
    Walled France —

André Gill was forerunner
to André Gide —
Long walks reading poems
in the Genet Haystacks —
The Voyant is born,
the deranged seer makes his
    first Manifesto,
gives vowels colors
    & consonants carking care,
comes under the influence
of old French Fairies
who accuse him of constipation
of the brain & diarrhea
    of the mouth —
Verlaine summons him to Paris
with less aplomb than he
did banish girls to
    Abyssinia —

"Merde!" screams Rimbaud
at Verlaine salons —
Gossip in Paris — Verlaine Wife
is jealous of a boy
with no seats to his trousers
— Love sends money from Brussels
— Mother Rimbaud hates
the importunity of Madame
Veraline — Degenerate Arthur
    is suspected of being a poet
        by now —
Screaming in the barn
    Rimbaud writes Season in Hell,
his mother trembles —
Verlaine sends money & bullets
    into Rimbaud —
    Rimbaud goes to the police
    & presents his innocence
    like the pale innocence
    of his divine, feminine Jesus
— Poor Verlaine, 2 years
in the can, but could have
got a knife in the heart

— Illuminations! Stuttgart!
Study of Languages!
On foot Rimbaud walks
& looks thru the Alpine
passes into Italy, looking

34

for clover bells, rabbits,
Genie Kingdoms & ahead
of him nothing but the old
    Canaletto death of sun
    on old Venetian buildings
— Rimbaud studies language
— hears of the Alleghanies,
of Brooklyn, of last
    American Plages —
His angel sister dies —
    Vienne! He looks at pastries
    & pets old dogs! I hope!
This mad cat joins
    the Dutch Army
    & sails for Java
commanding the fleet
    at midnight
    on the bow, alone,
    no one hears his Command
but every fishy shining
    in the sea — August is no
time to stay in Java —
    Aiming at Egypt, he's again
hungup in Italy so he goes
back home to deep armchair
but immediately he goes
again, to Cyprus, to
    run a gang of quarry

workers, — what did he
    look like now, this Later
    Rimbaud? — Rock dust
& black backs & hacks
    of coughers, the dream rises
in the Frenchman's Africa
mind, — Invalids from
  the tropics are always
    loved — The Red Sea
    in June, the coast clanks
    of Arabia — Havar,
    Havar, the magic trading
    post — Aden, Aden,
      South of Bedouin —
      Ogaden, Ogaden, never
      known — (Meanwhile
      Verlaine sits in Paris
  over cognacs wondering
what Arthur looks like
  now, & how bleak their
eyebrows because they believed
in earlier eyebrow beauty —
Who cares? What kinda
Frenchmen are these?
Rimbaud, hit me over the
head with that rock!

Serious Rimbaud composes
elegant & learned articles
for National Geographic
Societies, & after wars
commands Harari Girl
(Ha <u>Ha</u> !) back
to Abyssinia, & she
was young, had black
    eyes, thick lips, hair
    curled, & breasts like
    polished brown with
    copper teats & ringlets
    on her arms & joined
      her hands upon her
      central loin & had
      shoulders as broad as
      Arthur's, & little ears
— A girl of some
    caste, in Bronzeville —

    Rimbaud also knew
thinbonehipped Polynesians
with long tumbling hair
  & tiny tits & big feet

—

    Finally he starts
trading illegal guns

in Tajoura
riding in caravans, mad,
with a belt of gold
around his waist —
Screwed by King Menelek!
The Shah of Shoa!
The noises of these names
in that noisy French
mind!

Cairo for the summer,
bitter lemon wind
& kisses in the dusty park
where girls sit folded
at dusk thinking
nothing —

Havar! Havar!
By litter to Zeyla
he's carried moaning his
birthday — the boat
returns to chalk castle
Marseilles sadder than
time, than dream,
sadder than water
— Carcinoma, Rimbaud
is eaten by the disease
of overlife — They cut
off his beautiful leg —

He dies in the arms
   of Ste. Isabelle
      his sister
& before rising to Heaven
sends his francs
   to Djami, Djami
      the Havari boy
         his body servant
         8 years in the African
         Frenchman's Hell,
         & it all adds up
            to nothing, like

      Dostoevsky, Beethoven
         or Da Vinci —
So, poets, rest awhile
   & shut up:
Nothing ever came
   of nothing.

1960

from OLD ANGEL MIDNIGHT

54.

peep
peep the
bird tear the
sad bird drop heart
the dawn has slung
he aw arrow drape

to sissyfoo & made eastpink
dink the dimple solstice men
crut and so the birds go ttleep
and now bird number two three four five
six seven and seven million of em den
dead bens barking   now the birds are yakking
& barking swinging Crack! Wow! Quiet! the
birds are making an awful racket in the Row
tweep? tswip!   creet! clink! crack!
ding   dong   the bell   rope   bird of break of day
O k a y   b i r d s   q u i e t
p l e a s e

you birds
robins
black & blue birds

40

redbreasts & all
sisters, ————

my little parents
have the morning
by the golden balls

And over there the sultan forgot

1959

MORE OLD ANGEL MIDNIGHT

Old Angel Midnight the swan of heaven fell
      and flew cockmeek
Old Angel Midnight the night onta twelve
        Year Tart with the long bing bong
        and the big ding dong
The boy on the sandbank blooming the moon,
The sound won't let me sleep and since I
        found out time is silence Manjusri won't
        let me hear the swash of snow no mo
        in ole no po
O A M
Oh O M
The old Midnacker snacker tired a twit twit twit
        the Mc Tarty long true
The yentence peak peck slit slippymeek twang
        twall I'd heerd was flip the hand curse
        lead pencil in the shaky desk
Ah ow HURT!
Tantapalii the silken tont retchy swan
        bent necky I wish I had enuf sense to swim
        as I hear
O lousy tired gal
One more!
Choired arranged silence singers imbibing
        belly blum

Wreck the high charch chichipa and get firm
        juicy thebest thebest no other oil
        has ever heard such peanut squeeze
On top of which you yold yang midnockitwatter
        lying there in baid imagining casbah concepts
        from a highland fling moorish beach
        by moonlight medallion indicative spidergirls
        with sand legs waiting for the non-Christian
        cock, come O World window Wowf
& BARK!
   BARK!
   BARK for the girls of Tranatat
Because by the time those two Mominuan monks
        with girls & boys in their matted hair pans
        sense wind in the flower the golden lord will
        turn the imbecile himself into slip paper
Or dog paper
Or that pipe blend birds never peck because
        their bills are too hard
That window paper

1961

43

Auro Boralis Shomoheen
In the ancient blue Buick
Machine that cankers the highway
With Alice fed Queens, cards
Indexes burning, mapping machines,
Parting's sweet sorrow
But O my patine

O my patinat pinkplat Mexican
Canvas for oil in boil
Marrico — has marsh m draw
The greenhouse bong eater from
fence N'awrleans, that —

Bat and be ready, Jesus is steady,
Score's eight to one, none,
Bone was the batter for McGoy
Poy —
            Used as this ditties
            for mopping the kitties
            in dream's afternoon
            when nap was a drape.

1953?

LONG DEAD'S LONGEVITY

Long dead's longevity
Coyote Viejo
Ugly un handsome old
    puff chin eye crack
Bone fat face McGee
In older rains sat by
    new fires
Plotting unwanted pre
    doomed presupposing
Odes — long dead
Riverbottom bum
Raunchy
Scrounge
Brakeman bum
Wine cans sand sexless
    Silence die tomb
Pyramid cave snake Satan

1952?

SITTING UNDER TREE NUMBER TWO

But the undrawables,
  the single musical harp
rainbow's blue green
shimmer of a cobweb —
the line of thread swimming
in the wind, blue &
silver at intervals that
appear & disappear —
7 songe along the rim
tying to the plant
as birds twurdle over
those massy fort trees
populous with song
— imaginary blossoms in my
eye moving across the
page with definite oily
rainbow water holes &
rims of beaten gold,
  with toads of old
          silver.
Golden fast ant back
in the hay now fromming
its feelers thru the
thicket of time then
darting across mud looking
for more trees —

A little ant bit my ass
& I said Eeesh with
my wad of gum — I
itch & pain all over
with hate of time &
tedium Save me!
   Kill me!

1959

A CURSE AT THE DEVIL

Lucifer Sansfoi
  Varlet Sansfoi

  Omer Perdieu
   I. B. Perdie
    Billy Perdy

I'll unwind your
  guts from Durham
    to Dover
    and bury em
    in Clover —

Your psalms I'll 'ave
  engraved
  in your toothbone —

Your victories
nilled —
You jailed uner
a woman's skirt   .
    of stone —

Stone blind woman
with no guts
and only a scale —

Your thoughts & letters
Shandy'd about
in <u>Beth</u>
(Gaelic for <u>grave</u>).

Your philosophies
run up your nose
again —

Your confidences
and essays bandied
in ballrooms
from switchblade
to switchblade

— Your final
duel with
sledge hammers —
Your essential
secret twinned
to buttercups
& dying

Your guide to 32
European cities
scabbed in Isaiah
— Your red beard
snobbed in

49

Dolmen ruins
in the editions
of the Bleak —

Your saints and
Consolations bereft
— Your handy volume
rolled into
        an urn —

And your father
  and mother besmeared
  at thought of you
  th'unspent begotless
    crop of worms
— You lay
  there, you
  queen for a
  day, wait
for the "fen-
  sucked fogs"
  to carp at you

Your sweety beauty
discovered by No Name
in its hidingplace

  til burrs
part from you

from lack
of issue,
  sinew, all
  the rest —
Gibbering quiver
  graveyard HOO!

  The hospital
that buries you
    be Baal,
  the digger
  Yorrick
& the shoveler
  groom —

My rosy tomatoes
pop squirting
  from your awful
  rotten grave —

Your profile,
  erstwhile
    Garboesque,
  mistook by earth —
  eels for some
    fjord to
      Sheol —

And your timid
  voice box
  strangled
  by lie-hating
    earth
      forever.

May the plighted
  Noah-clouds
    dissolve in grief
    of you —

May Red clay
  be your center
& woven into necks
  of hogs, boars,
  booters & pilferers
  & burned down
  with Stalin, Hitler
  & the rest —

May you bite
your lip that
  you cannot
  meet with God —
    or
Beat me to a pub
      — Amen

The Almoner,
  his cup hath
    no bottom,
  nor I
    a brim.

Devil, get thee
back
  to russet caves.

1965

Sight is just dust,
Obey it must.

Fire just feeds
On fiery deeds.

Water from the moon
Appears very soon.

Wind in the trees
Is a mental breeze.

Space in the ground
Was dirt by the pound.

Mind alone
Introduced the bone.

Only mind
The flame so kind.

Mind is the sea
Made water agree.

Wind rose deep
From empty sleep.

Devoid of space
Is the mind of grace.

1955?

POEM

How'd they ever get that tap
    outa me?
Wasnt I tired givin?
    hard tap
Family tree.

I wasnt sweet givin.

1955?

TO EDWARD DAHLBERG

Don't use the telephone.
People are never ready to answer it.
Use poetry.

1970

TWO POEMS

Wee wee wee poem
    angel smoke
We wee not-worth-reading
    little poem

You start off by suckin in
    milk
And you end up suckin in
    smoke

And you know
What milk and smoke
Denote

1957

TO ALLEN GINSBERG

Usta smear ma lips with whiskey
  Fred and open up the doors
  to make a joke — while
    women waited
    and Bert Lahr waited
    playing what he wanted
    like Duke Ellington

used to sit staring at Seymour
who implied to me the swing
  of the music by his
      low crash
      high abidin
                shoulders,
          Pap,
    and what how who?

T H O T H A T N A P E

    Compose Vehicle
      Special
      Banana
      Nine

1959

57

POEM

Jazz killed itself
But dont let poetry kill itself

Dont be afraid
  of the cold night air

Dont listen to institutions
when you return manuscripts to
    brownstone

dont bow & scuffle
        for Edith Wharton pioneers
or ursula major nebraska prose
  just hang in your own backyard
    & laugh play pretty
        cake trombone
& if somebody give you beads
  juju, jew, or otherwise,

sleep with em around your neck

Your dreams'll maybe better

    There's no rain
        there's no me,
    I'm tellin ya man
        sure as shit.
1959

TO HARPO MARX

O Harpo! When did you seem like an angel
   the last time?
   and played the gray harp of gold?

When did you steal the silverware
   and bug-spray the guests?

When did your brother find rain
   in your sunny courtyard?

When did you chase your last blonde
   across the Millionairesses' lawn
   with a bait hook on a line
   protruding from your bicycle?

Or when last you powderpuffed
   your white flour face
   with fishbarrel cover?

Harpo! Who was that Lion
   I saw you with?

How did you treat the midget
   and Konk the giant?

Harpo, in your recent night-club appearance
   in New Orleans were you old?

Were you still chiding with your horn
in the cane at your golden belt?

Did you still emerge from your pockets
another Harpo, or screw on
new wrists?

Was your vow of silence an Indian Harp?

1959

HITCH HIKER

"Tryna get to sunny Californy" ——
    Boom. It's the awful raincoat
making me look like a selfdefeated self-
murdering imaginary gangster, an idiot in
a rueful coat, how can they understand
my damp packs—my mud packs—
        "Look Joh, a hitchhiker"
        "He looks like he's got a gun underneath
that I.R.A. coat"
        "Look Fred, that man by the road"
        "Some sexfiend got in print in 1938
in Sex Magazine"——
        "You found his blue corpse in a
greenshade edition, with axe blots"

1967

FOUR POEMS from "SAN FRANCISCO BLUES"

1
The rooftop of the beatup
tenement
on 3rd & Harrison
has Belfast painted
black on yellow
on the side
the old Frisco wood is
shown with weatherbeaten
rainboards, & a
washed out blue bottle
once painted for wild
commercial reasons by
an excited seltzerite
as firemen came last
afternoon & raised the
ladder to a fruitless
fire that was not there,
so, is Belfast singing
        in this time
when brand's forgotten
taste washed in
rain the gullies broadened
and everybody gone
and acrobats of the
        tenement
        who dug bel fast

divers all
and the divers all dove
ah
little girls make
shadows on the
sidewalk shorter
than the shadow
of death
in this town —

2
Somewhere in this snow
I see little children raped
By maniacal sex fiends
Eager to make a break
But the F.B.I.
In the form of Ted
Stands waiting
Hand on gun
In the Paranoiac
Summer time
To come.

3
Eccentrics from out of town
Better not fill in
this blank
For a job on my gray boat
And Monkeysuits I furnish.

Sober serious
Marcelle-waved
Heroes only.

4
And
The taste of worms
Is soft & salty
Like the sea
Or tears.

1961

from SAN FRANCISCO BLUES

13

This pretty white city
On the other side of the country
Will no longer be
Available to me
I saw heaven move
Said 'This is the end'
Because I was tired
of all that portend
And any time you need
  me
Call
  I'll be at the other
        end
Waiting
  at the final wall

14

San Francisco Blues
Written in a rocking chair
In the Cameo Hotel
San Francisco Skid row
Nineteen Fifty Four

1957

BLUES

And he sits embrowned
  in a brown chest
Before the palish priests

And he points delicately
  at the sky
With palm and forefinger

And's got a halo
  of gate black

And's got a hawknosed
  watcher who loves to hate

But has learned to meditate
  It do no good to hate

So watches, roseate laurel
  on head
In back of Prince Avalokitesvar
  Who moos with snow hand
And laces with pearls
  the sea's majesty

1959

66

BLUES

Part of the morning stars
  The moon and the mail
The ravenous X, the raving ache,
— the moon Sittle La
Pottle, teh, teh, teh, —

  The poets in owlish old rooms
  who write bent over words
  know that words were invented
  because nothing was nothing

In use of words, use words,
the X and the blank
And the Emperor's white page
And the last of the Bulls
Before spring operates
Are all lotsa nothin
  which we got anyway
So we'll deal in the night
  in the market of words

1959

Hey listen you poetry audiences
If you dont shut up
And listen to the potry,
See . . we'll set a guy at the gate
To bar all potry haters
Forevermore

Then, if you dont like the subject
Of the poem that the poit
Is readin, geen, why dont
You try Marlon Brando
Who'll open your eyes
With his cry

James Dean is dead? ——
   Aint we all?
   Who aint dead ——

John Barrymore is dead

Naw San Francisco is dead
— San Francisco is bleat
   With the fog

1956?

SOME WESTERN HAIKUS

EXPLANATORY NOTE BY AUTHOR: The "Haiku" was in-
vented and developed over hundreds of years in Japan to be a
complete poem in seventeen syllables and to pack in a whole vi-
sion of life in three short lines. A "Western Haiku" need not
concern itself with the seventeen syllables since Western lan-
guages cannot adapt themselves to the fluid syllabillic Japanese.
I propose that the "Western Haiku" simply say a lot in three
short lines in any Western language.

Above all, a Haiku must be very simple and free of all po-
etic trickery and make a little picture and yet be as airy and
graceful as a Vivaldi Pastorella. Here is a great Japanese Haiku
that is simpler and prettier than any Haiku I could ever write
in any language:—

> A day of quiet gladness,—
> Mount Fuji is veiled
> In misty rain.
>
> (Basho) (1644-1694)

Here is another:

> Nesetsukeshi ko no
> Sentaku ya natsu
> No tsuki

> She has put the child to sleep,
> And now washes the clothes;
> The summer moon.
> (Issa) (1763-1827)

And another, by Buson (1715-1783):

> The nightingale is singing,
> Its small mouth
> Open.

SOME WESTERN HAIKUS

Jack Kerouac

* * *

Arms folded
  to the moon,
Among the cows.

Birds singing
  in the dark
— Rainy dawn.

Elephants munching
  on grass — loving
Heads side by side.

Missing a kick
  at the icebox door
It closed anyway.

Perfect moonlit night
  marred
By family squabbles.

This July evening,
  a large frog
On my door sill.

Catfish fighting for his life,
  and winning,
Splashing us all.

Evening coming —
  the office girl
Unloosing her scarf.

The low yellow
  moon above the
Quiet lamplit house

Shall I say no?
  - fly rubbing
its back legs

Unencouraging sign
  — the fish store
Is closed.

Nodding against
  the wall, the flowers
Sneeze

72

Straining at the padlock,
    the garage doors
At noon

The taste
  of rain
— Why kneel?

The moon,
    the falling star
— Look elsewhere

The rain has filled
  the birdbath
Again, almost

And the quiet cat
    sitting by the post
Perceives the moon

Useless, useless,
  the heavy rain
Driving into the sea.

Juju beads on the
    Zen Manual:
My knees are cold.

73

Those birds sitting
   out there on the fence —
They're all going to die.

The bottoms of my shoes
   are wet
from walking in the rain

In my medicine cabinet,
   the winter fly
has died of old age.

November — how nasal
   the drunken
Conductor's call

The moon had
   a cat's mustache
For a second

A big fat flake
   of snow
Falling all alone

The summer chair
   rocking by itself
In the blizzard

— from **BOOK OF HAIKU**

SOURCES

A Translation From The French (Jester of Columbia, 1945)
Song: Fie My fum (Neurotica 1950)
Pull My Daisy (Evergreen Books 1961)
Pull My Daisy (Metronome April 1961)
He is your friend (Letter to Ginsberg 1952)
Old buddy (Ginsberg 1956?)
Daydreams for Ginsberg (Letter to Ginsberg 1955)
Lucien Midnight (Combustion April 1957)
Someday you'll be lying (Kriya Broadside 1968)
I clearly saw (New Departures 1960)
Hymn (Pax 1959)
Poem: I demand (Pax 1962)
The Thrashing Doves (White Dove Review 1959)
The Buddhist Saints (Letter to Ginsberg 1956)
How to Meditate (Floating Bear 1967)
A Pun for Al Gelpi (Lowell House Printers 1966)
Sept. 16, 1961 (The Outsider 1962)
Rimbaud (Yugen 1960; City Lights)
from Old Angel Midnight (Beetitood 1959)
More Old Angel Midnight (New Directions 1961)
Auro Boralis Shomoheen (Letter to Ginsberg 1955?)
Long Dead's Longevity (Letter to Ginsberg 1952?)
Sitting Under Tree#2 (Yugen 1959)
A Curse At The Devil (Red Clay Reader 1965)
Sight is just dust (Letter to Ginsberg 1955)

POEM (Letter to Ginsberg 1955?)
To Edward Dahlberg (TriQuarterly 1970)
Two Poems (Combustion 1957)
To Allen Ginsberg (White Dove Review 1959)
Poem: Jazz Killed Itself (White Dove Review 1959)
To Harpo Marx (Playboy 1959)
Hitch Hiker (Floating Bear 1967)
4 Poems from S. F. Blues (New Directions 1961)
from S. F. Blues (Ark 1957)
Blues: And he sits embrowned (Yugen 1959)
Blues: Part of the morning stars (Yugen 1959)
Hey listen you poetry audiences (Letter to Ginsberg 1956)
Some Western Haikus (Ginsberg, Yugen, Beetitude, Bussei,
  Portents 1956-1968)

Dates following the poems indicate year of publication, not
necessarily composition. Dates followed by a question mark
are approximate year of composition.

CITY LIGHTS PUBLICATIONS

Allen, Roberta. AMAZON DREAM
Angulo de, Jaime. INDIANS IN OVERALLS
Angulo de, G. & J. de Angulo. JAIME IN TAOS
Artaud, Antonin. ARTAUD ANTHOLOGY
Bataille, Georges. EROTISM: Death and Sensuality
Bataille, Georges. THE IMPOSSIBLE
Bataille, Georges. STORY OF THE EYE
Bataille, Georges. THE TEARS OF EROS
Baudelaire, Charles. TWENTY PROSE POEMS
Baudelaire, Charles. INTIMATE JOURNALS
Bowles, Paul. A HUNDRED CAMELS IN THE COURTYARD
Broughton, James. MAKING LIGHT OF IT
Brown, Rebecca. THE TERRIBLE GIRLS
Bukowski, Charles. THE MOST BEAUTIFUL WOMAN IN TOWN
Bukowski, Charles. NOTES OF A DIRTY OLD MAN
Bukowski, Charles. TALES OF ORDINARY MADNESS
Burroughs, William S. THE BURROUGHS FILE
Burroughs, William S. THE YAGE LETTERS
Cassady, Neal. THE FIRST THIRD
Choukri, Mohamed. FOR BREAD ALONE
CITY LIGHTS REVIEW #1: Politics and Poetry issue
CITY LIGHTS REVIEW #2: AIDS & the Arts forum
CITY LIGHTS REVIEW #3: Media and Propaganda issue
CITY LIGHTS REVIEW #4: Literature / Politics / Ecology
Cocteau, Jean. THE WHITE BOOK (LE LIVRE BLANC)
Codrescu, Andrei, ed. EXQUISITE CORPSE READER
Cornford, Adam. ANIMATIONS
Corso, Gregory. GASOLINE
Daumal, Réne. THE POWERS OF THE WORD
David-Neel, Alexandra. SECRET ORAL TEACHINGS IN TIBETAN BUDDHIST SECTS
Deleuze, Gilles. SPINOZA: Practical Philosophy
Dick, Leslie. WITHOUT FALLING
di Prima, Diane. PIECES OF A SONG: Selected Poems
H. D. (Hilda Doolittle). NOTES ON THOUGHT & VISION
Ducornet, Rikki. ENTERING FIRE
Duras, Marguerite. DURAS BY DURAS

Eidus, Janice. VITO LOVES GERALDINE
Eberhardt, Isabelle. THE OBLIVION SEEKERS
Ferlinghetti, Lawrence. PICTURES OF THE GONE WORLD
Ferlinghetti, Lawrence. SEVEN DAYS IN NICARAGUA LIBRE
Finley, Karen. SHOCK TREATMENT
Ford, Charles Henri. OUT OF THE LABYRINTH: Selected Poems
Franzen, Cola, transl. POEMS OF ARAB ANDALUSIA
García Lorca, Federico. BARBAROUS NIGHTS: Legends & Plays
García Lorca, Federico. ODE TO WALT WHITMAN & OTHER POEMS
García Lorca, Federico. POEM OF THE DEEP SONG
Ginsberg, Allen. HOWL & OTHER POEMS
Ginsberg, Allen. KADDISH & OTHER POEMS
Ginsberg, Allen. REALITY SANDWICHES
Ginsberg, Allen. PLANET NEWS
Ginsberg, Allen. THE FALL OF AMERICA
Ginsberg, Allen. MIND BREATHS
Ginsberg, Allen. PLUTONIAN ODE
Goethe, J. W. von. TALES FOR TRANSFORMATION
Hayton-Keeva, Sally, ed. VALIANT WOMEN IN WAR AND EXILE
Herron, Don. THE DASHIELL HAMMETT TOUR: A Guidebook
Herron, Don. THE LITERARY WORLD OF SAN FRANCISCO
Higman, Perry, tr. LOVE POEMS FROM SPAIN AND SPANISH AMERICA
Jaffe, Harold. EROS: Anti-Eros
Jenkins, Edith. AGAINST A FIELD SINISTER
Kerouac, Jack. BOOK OF DREAMS
Kerouac, Jack. POMES ALL SIZES
Kerouac, Jack. SCATTERED POEMS
Lacarrière, Jacques. THE GNOSTICS
La Duke, Betty. COMPANERAS: Women, Art & Social Change in Latin America
La Loca. ADVENTURES ON THE ISLE OF ADOLESCENCE
Lamantia, Philip. MEADOWLARK WEST
Lamantia, Philip. BECOMING VISIBLE
Laughlin, James. SELECTED POEMS: 1935-1985
Le Brun, Annie. SADE: On the Brink of the Abyss
Lowry, Malcolm. SELECTED POEMS
Marcelin, Philippe-Thoby. THE BEAST OF THE HAITIAN HILLS
Masereel, Frans. PASSIONATE JOURNEY
Mayakovsky, Vladimir. LISTEN! EARLY POEMS
Mrabet, Mohammed. THE BOY WHO SET THE FIRE

Mrabet, Mohammed. THE LEMON
Mrabet, Mohammed. LOVE WITH A FEW HAIRS
Mrabet, Mohammed. M'HASHISH
Murguia, A. & B. Paschke, eds. VOLCAN: Poems from Central America
Murillo, Rosario. ANGEL IN THE DELUGE
Paschke, B. & D. Volpendesta, eds. CLAMOR OF INNOCENCE
Pessoa, Fernando. ALWAYS ASTONISHED
Peters, Nancy J., ed. WAR AFTER WAR (City Lights Review #5)
Pasolini, Pier Paolo. ROMAN POEMS
Poe, Edgar Allan. THE UNKNOWN POE
Porta, Antonio. KISSES FROM ANOTHER DREAM
Purdy, James. THE CANDLES OF YOUR EYES
Purdy, James. IN A SHALLOW GRAVE
Purdy, James. GARMENTS THE LIVING WEAR
Prévert, Jacques. PAROLES
Rachlin, Nahid. VEILS: SHORT STORIES
Rey Rosa, Rodrigo. THE BEGGAR'S KNIFE
Rey Rosa, Rodrigo. DUST ON HER TONGUE
Rigaud, Milo. SECRETS OF VOODOO
Saadawi El, Nawal. MEMOIRS OF A WOMAN DOCTOR
Sánchez, Alberto Ruy. MOGADOR
Sawyer-Lauçanno, Christopher, transl. THE DESTRUCTION OF THE JAGUAR
Sclauzero, Mariarosa. MARLENE
Serge, Victor. RESISTANCE
Shepard, Sam. MOTEL CHRONICLES
Shepard, Sam. FOOL FOR LOVE & THE SAD LAMENT OF PECOS BILL
Smith, Michael. IT A COME
Snyder, Gary. THE OLD WAYS
Solnit, Rebecca. SECRET EXHIBITION: Six California Artists of the Cold War Era
Sussler, Betsy, ed. BOMB: INTERVIEWS
Takahashi, Mutsuo. SLEEPING SINNING FALLING
Turyn, Anne, ed. TOP TOP STORIES
Tutuola, Amos. FEATHER WOMAN OF THE JUNGLE
Tutuola, Amos. SIMBI & THE SATYR OF THE DARK JUNGLE
Valaoritis, Nanos. MY AFTERLIFE GUARANTEED
Wilson, Colin. POETRY AND MYSTICISM
Zamora, Daisy. RIVERBED OF MEMORY